Beadlings™

How to Make Beaded
Creatures & Creations

by Julie Collings & Candice Elton

KLUTZ

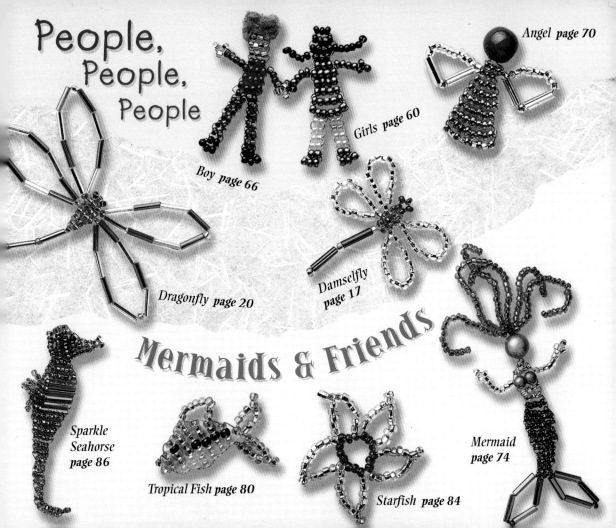

People, People, People

Boy **page 66**

Girls **page 60**

Angel **page 70**

Dragonfly **page 20**

Damselfly **page 17**

Mermaids & Friends

Sparkle Seahorse **page 86**

Tropical Fish **page 80**

Starfish **page 84**

Mermaid **page 74**

What you get with this book:

a super-cool, handy-dandy bead wheel to store your beads

8 mm wonder beads (for the angel and the mermaid's head)

4 mm wonder beads (for the eyes of the baby tree frog)

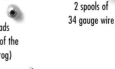

2 spools of 34 gauge wire

4 mm wonder beads (for the eyes of the giant tree frog)

size 4 bugle bead

size 10 seed bead

Other household items you'll need:

A ruler to measure out your wire and a pair of scissors or nail clippers to cut your wire. (Don't use your mom or dad's best pair!)

What if I need more beads or wire? Search out your local bead store or craft store to find more wire and beads. Or you can order more stuff through the Klutz Catalog. (See catalog request card on last page.)

Read This Stuff First!

Your Very First Project

Start by making the first project in the book: **The Buzz BEE**. It'll teach you the Back & Forth beading technique that's used throughout the book.

Crinkly Wire?

When your wire looks like this...

Clip here.

use scissors or nail clippers to clip the end to make beading easier.

Avoid Kinks!

Kinks in your wire can make beading difficult. Straighten them out before beading on.

Try to avoid this.

Threading Beads with Ease

Start each project by cutting the length of wire needed. Poke the wire end into the bead and slide the bead up the wire with your fingers.

Look for the Tips!

There are helpful hints strategically placed throughout the book. They'll help make the projects easier for you.

So, what can I do with my beadlings after I've made them?

There are so many different things you can do with your beadling creations. Here are just a few:

Use them as necklace or bracelet charms

Glue them to a headband

Make them into hair clips

Glue them to a picture frame

Attach them to gift tags

Make them into decorative pins

Create bookmarks with them

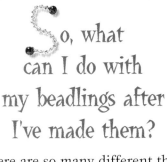

6

A Note from the Authors

The idea for this book came from our own kids. They started making beadlings to give to their friends at school. Soon we were making patterns for everything. Let your imagination go wild and create your own beadling designs.

FLIGHTY BUGS

Buzz BEE

This project teaches the basic Back & Forth beading technique.

Once you learn this, you can do all the projects in this book with ease!

row 1

String one black seed bead on the center of a 20″ wire.

Thread wire **B** back through the bead as shown.

A

B

Pull both wire ends to snug the wire loop around the bead.

A   B

Pull snug.

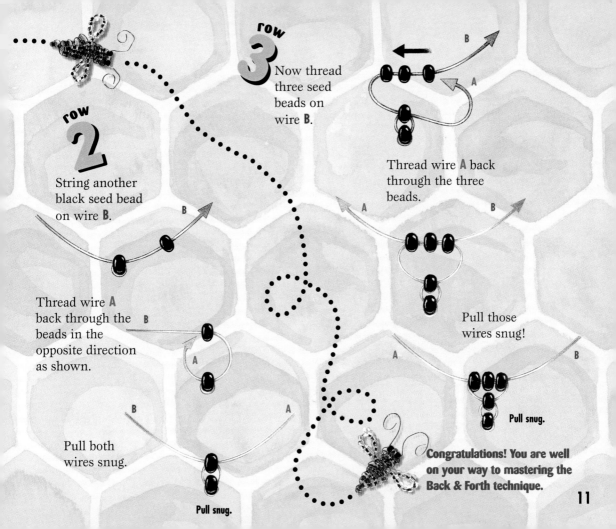

String another black seed bead on wire **B**.

Thread wire **A** back through the beads in the opposite direction as shown.

Pull both wires snug.

Pull snug.

Now thread three seed beads on wire **B**.

Thread wire **A** back through the three beads.

Pull those wires snug!

Pull snug.

Congratulations! You are well on your way to mastering the Back & Forth technique.

11

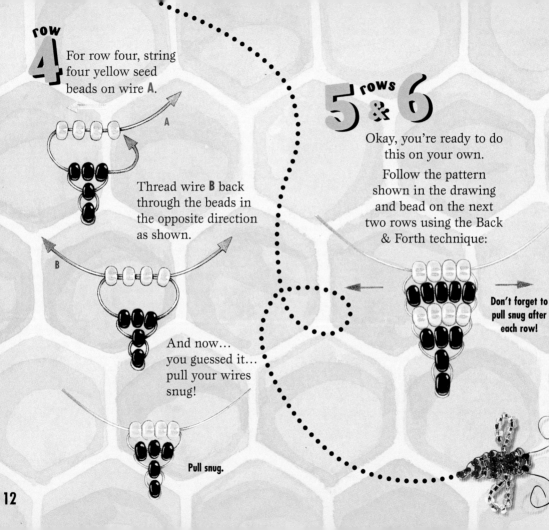

For row four, string four yellow seed beads on wire **A**.

Thread wire **B** back through the beads in the opposite direction as shown.

And now... you guessed it... pull your wires snug!

Pull snug.

rows **5** & **6**

Okay, you're ready to do this on your own.

Follow the pattern shown in the drawing and bead on the next two rows using the Back & Forth technique:

Don't forget to pull snug after each row!

12

the wings

String 12 clear seed beads on wire **A**. Thread the end of the wire back through the first bead as shown. Pull snug. Repeat on the other side.

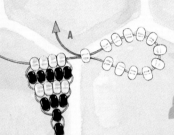

Hold the first wing bead next to the body as you pull the wire snug.

TIP

the finishing touch

String three black seed beads on wire **A**. Thread wire **B** through the beads in the opposite direction.

Pull snug.

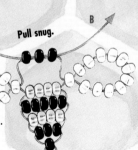

Using the Back & Forth technique, bead two more rows following the pattern below. Finish with antennae or a pendant loop.

For the pendant loop, loop both wires, thread the ends through a bead and secure by twisting.

Curl the wire ends around a toothpick to make the antennae.

1 String one seed bead on the center of a 24″ wire. Thread wire **B** back through the bead as shown.

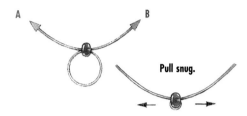

A

B

Pull snug.

2 String three seed beads on wire **A**. Thread wire **B** back through the beads in the opposite direction as shown. Do this twice.

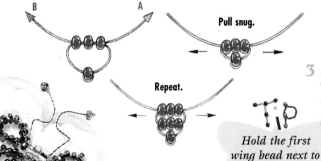

B

A

Pull snug.

Repeat.

Hold the first wing bead next to the body as you pull the wire snug.

3 String ten seed beads on wire **A**. Thread the end of the wire back through the first wing beads as shown. Pull snug. Repeat on wire **B**.

A

Repeat on the other side.

Baby

utterfly

7 Add a bead on wire **B**. Thread the wire end back through the last row. Pull the wire until the antenna is the length you want. Twist the bead around until tight. Clip off the extra wire. Do the same to the other side.

Twist.

B

Clip.

6 Add another row of three seed beads following this pattern:

5 To make the upper wings repeat step 3 only this time string on 12 seed beads. Do this on both sides.

4 Add another row of three seed beads.

Pull snug.

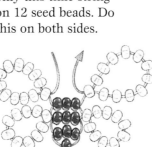

Damselfly

1 String five seed beads on the center of a 24″ wire following the color pattern. Thread wire **A** back through the two beads.

2 String three turquoise seed beads on wire **A**. Thread wire **B** through the beads in the opposite direction.

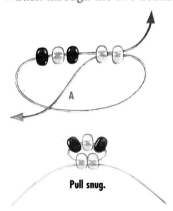

Pull snug.

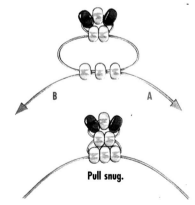

Pull snug.

3 String 20 clear seed beads on wire **A**. Thread the end of wire **A** back through the first bead as shown. Pull snug. Repeat for wire **B**.

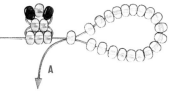

TiP

Hold the first wing bead next to the body as you pull the wire snug.

4 String three turquoise seed beads on wire **A**. Thread wire **B** through the beads the opposite direction. Pull snug.

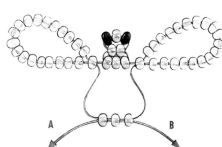

5 Repeat step 3 to make the second set of wings.

6 Using the Back & Forth technique, add one row of two turquoise beads.

7 Add the tail by stringing this pattern of beads onto both wires. Loop one wire around and through the last seed bead as shown. Hold tail close to the body as you pull snug.

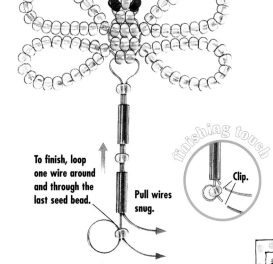

To finish, loop one wire around and through the last seed bead.

Pull wires snug.

finishing touch

Clip.

1 String six seed beads on the center of a 40″ wire following the color pattern. Thread wire Ⓐ back through the three beads as shown.

Pull snug.

Dragonfly Drago

String wing beads.

Ⓐ

2 String wing beads on wire Ⓐ following the color pattern above. Thread the end of wire Ⓐ back through the first seed bead as shown below. Pull snug. Repeat on the other side.

Ⓐ   Ⓑ

3 String four seed beads on wire Ⓐ. Thread wire Ⓑ through the beads in the opposite direction as shown. Pull snug.

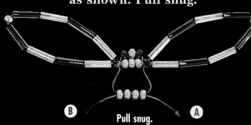

Ⓑ   Pull snug.   Ⓐ

4 Repeat step 2 for both wire Ⓐ and Ⓑ to create the second set of wings.

Ⓐ   Ⓑ

5 Using the Back & Forth technique, bead on the next four rows, following the pattern.

Pull snug
after each row.

Dragonfly

6

With both wires together, string on the tail beads following the pattern. Loop either wire Ⓐ or wire Ⓑ around and through the last seed bead as shown. Hold tail beads close to the body as you pull snug. Clip ends of wire to finish.

Ⓑ

Ⓐ

finishing touch

Clip.

21

1 Making the Bug Body

String eight seed beads on the center of a 20" wire.

Thread wire **A** back through five seed beads as shown.

A

B

Pull snug.

JEWEL
BUG

2

Using the Back & Forth technique, bead on the next six rows following the pattern.

Clip wire even and shape into antennae.

Don't forget to pull your wires snug after each row!

bead count
3
4
3
4
6
7

22

Adding the Wings

Cut a piece of 10" wire and thread it through two of the top body beads.

On the new wire, using the Back & Forth technique, make one row of two red beads.

Thread new wire through here.

Pull snug.

Bead on the next four rows following the color pattern. To end, thread wires back through the wing as shown. Clip extra wire.

Pull snug.

5

Repeat steps 3 and 4 for the other wing.

Now you're ready to fly!

Critters

in all colors

1 String one orange seed bead on the center of a 24″ wire. Thread wire **B** back through the bead as shown.

Pull snug.

LIZARD

2 String two orange seed beads on wire **A**. Thread wire **B** back through the beads as shown.

Pull snug.

3 Bead on the next three rows following this color pattern:

4 String three orange seed beads and three red seed beads on wire **A**.

A Thread beads on.

Loop wire **A** around the red beads and thread it back through the orange beads as shown.

A

Loop and thread wire back through.

Pull wire **A** snug.

Pull snug. **A**

To avoid having a gap between the leg and the body, slide the beads toward the body before you pull snug.

Repeat for wire **B**.

B

Pull snug.

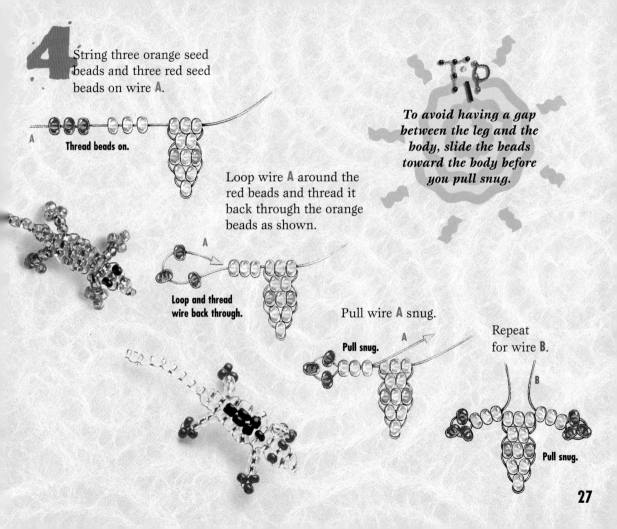

27

5 Bead on the next four rows following this color pattern:

6 Repeat step 4 to make the back legs.

28

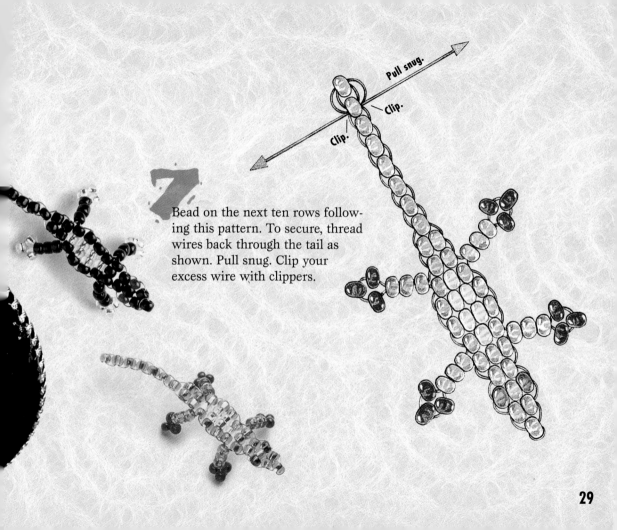

Bead on the next ten rows following this pattern. To secure, thread wires back through the tail as shown. Pull snug. Clip your excess wire with clippers.

Pull snug.

Clip.

Clip.

Whiffy Skunk

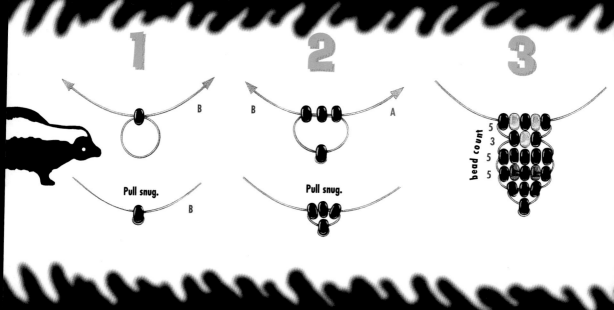

String one black seed bead on the center of a 24″ wire. Thread wire B back through the bead as shown.

String three black seed beads on wire A. Thread wire B back through the bead as shown.

Using the Back & Forth technique, bead on the next four rows following this color pattern.

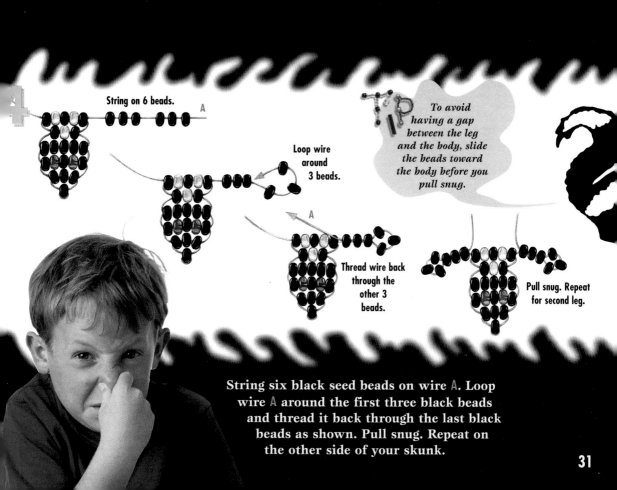

String on 6 beads.

A

Loop wire around 3 beads.

A

Thread wire back through the other 3 beads.

Pull snug. Repeat for second leg.

To avoid having a gap between the leg and the body, slide the beads toward the body before you pull snug.

String six black seed beads on wire A. Loop wire A around the first three black beads and thread it back through the last black beads as shown. Pull snug. Repeat on the other side of your skunk.

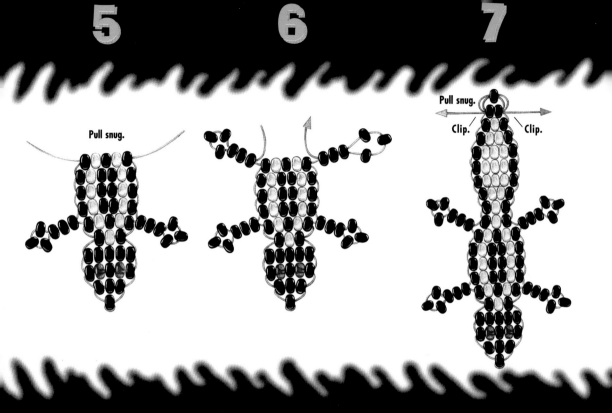

5

Using the Back & Forth technique bead on the next four rows following the color pattern above.

6

Repeat step 4 to make the back legs.

7

Using the Back & Forth technique, bead on the next ten rows following this pattern. To secure, thread both wires back through the tail as shown.

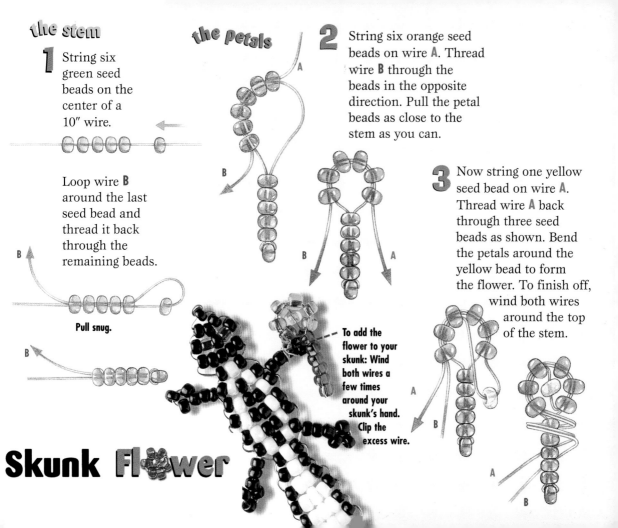

the stem

1 String six green seed beads on the center of a 10" wire.

Loop wire **B** around the last seed bead and thread it back through the remaining beads.

B

Pull snug.

B

the petals

A

B

2 String six orange seed beads on wire **A**. Thread wire **B** through the beads in the opposite direction. Pull the petal beads as close to the stem as you can.

B   **A**

3 Now string one yellow seed bead on wire **A**. Thread wire **A** back through three seed beads as shown. Bend the petals around the yellow bead to form the flower. To finish off, wind both wires around the top of the stem.

A
B

A

B

To add the flower to your skunk: Wind both wires a few times around your skunk's hand. Clip the excess wire.

Skunk Flower

Baby Tree Frog

1

String one seed bead and one small wonder bead on the center of a 20" wire. Loop wire **A** around the seed bead and back through the wonder bead.

Pull snug.

2

Repeat step 1 on wire **B**, but this time thread on the wonder bead first and then the seed bead.

End up like this with a little space between the two eyes.

3

Pull both wires snug so
the beads are centered
behind the eyes like this.

B ← → A

String five seed beads on
wire **A**. Thread wire **B**
through the beads in
the opposite direction
as shown.

4

To make the right leg, string 11
seed beads on wire **A**. Loop wire **A** around
the last three beads and back through the remaining
eight as shown. Pull the wire to snug beads close to
the frog body. Repeat for the left leg.

B

B

5

Using the Back & Forth technique, bead on the next four rows following the pattern. Don't forget to pull your wires snug after each row.

B   A

6

To make the back leg, string 15 seed beads on wire A. Loop wire around the last three beads and back through the 12 beads. Repeat for the second back leg. Clip the excess wire.

Clip.

Large Tree frog

1

Cut a piece of wire 36″ long. Thread one seed bead and one medium-sized wonder bead onto the center of the wire. Loop the end of wire **A** back through the wonder bead as shown.

Pull snug, keeping the beads centered on the wire.

For the other eye, thread a wonder bead and then a seed bead on wire **B**. Loop the wire back through the wonder bead.

End up like this with a little space between the eyes.

A   B

Using the Back & Forth technique, bead on the next two rows.

Tip

Pull each row **super tight.** It'll make your bead rows overlap.

Pull super snug to make your rows overlap.

3 String three seed beads, one bugle bead, one seed bead, another bugle bead and three more seed beads on wire **A** like this:

Loop the end of wire **A** around the last seed bead and string it back through two seed beads.

Pull snug.

String three more seed beads on wire **A**.

Loop wire **A** around the last seed bead and back through the other two beads.

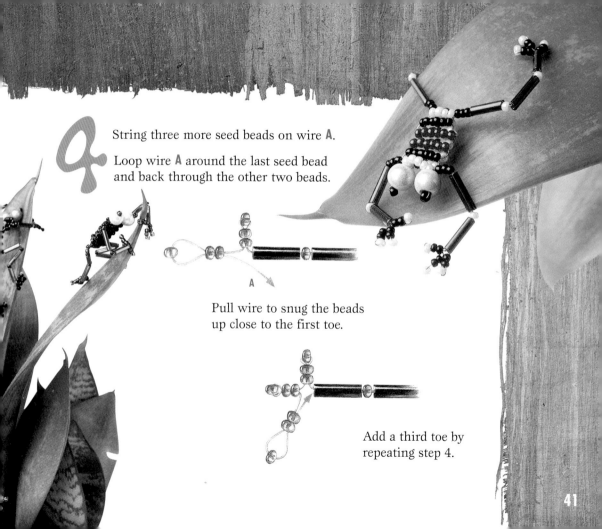

A

Pull wire to snug the beads up close to the first toe.

Add a third toe by repeating step 4.

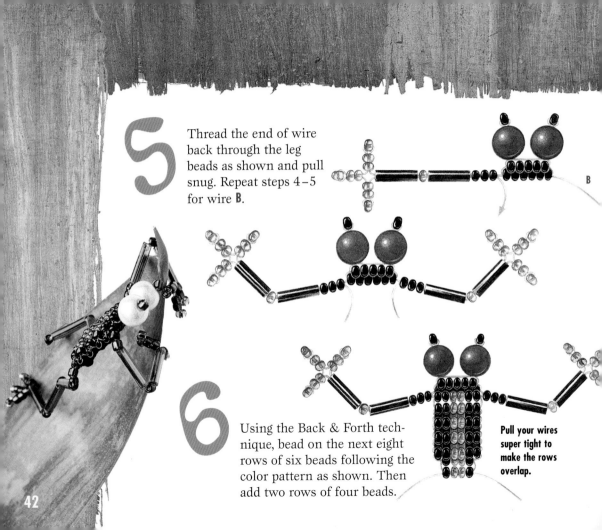

5 Thread the end of wire back through the leg beads as shown and pull snug. Repeat steps 4–5 for wire **B**.

B

6 Using the Back & Forth technique, bead on the next eight rows of six beads following the color pattern as shown. Then add two rows of four beads.

Pull your wires super tight to make the rows overlap.

Backlegs

To make the back legs, repeat steps 3–5, using more beads as shown. Don't forget to pull them snug.

Clip.

Use 4 beads for each toe.

Finishing Touch

Thread wire back through the first bugle bead. Clip the extra wire.

1 String eight seed beads on the center of a 40″ wire. Thread wire **A** back through the five beads as shown.

A

Pull snug.

2 Using the Back & Forth technique, bead on the next seven rows following the pattern.

bead count

3
4
6
7
8
8
7

*S*pider

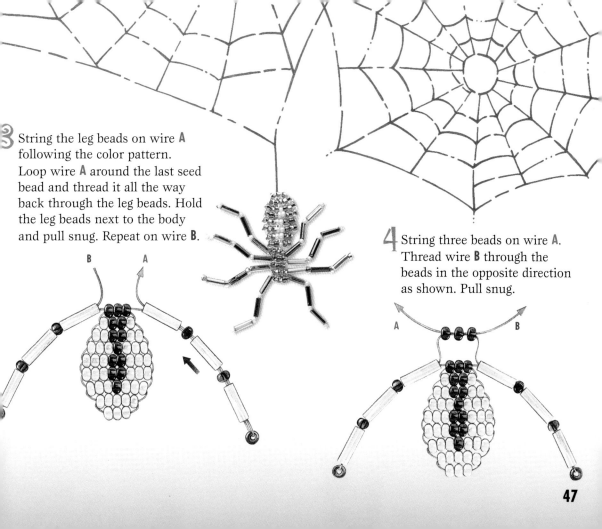

3 String the leg beads on wire **A** following the color pattern. Loop wire **A** around the last seed bead and thread it all the way back through the leg beads. Hold the leg beads next to the body and pull snug. Repeat on wire **B**.

4 String three beads on wire **A**. Thread wire **B** through the beads in the opposite direction as shown. Pull snug.

47

5 Repeat steps 3 and 4 three more times for all eight legs.

48

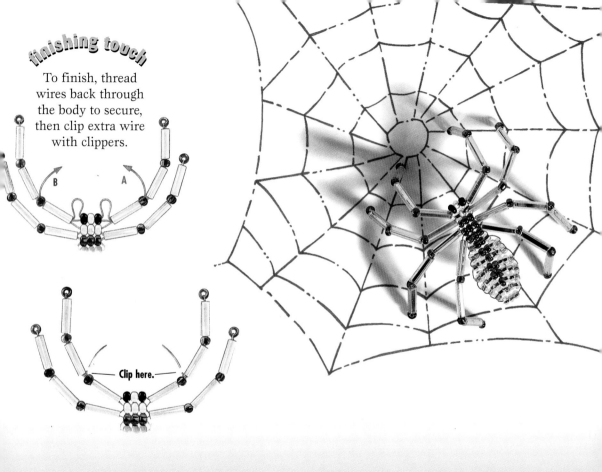

finishing touch

To finish, thread wires back through the body to secure, then clip extra wire with clippers.

B   A

Clip here.

49

1

String seven red seed beads on the center of a 36" wire. Thread wire **A** back through the four beads.

Pull snug.

2

Now string five red seed beads on wire **A**.

Thread wire **B** through the beads the opposite direction as shown.

Pull snug.

Dancin

3

bead count

3
3
4
5
6
6

Using the Back & Forth technique, bead on the next six rows, following the bead count.

4

The back legs are next. String on two bugle beads and three seed beads. Then loop the end of your wire around the last seed bead and thread it back through the rest of the leg beads. Hold the beads close to the body as you pull snug. Repeat to make the other leg.

ants

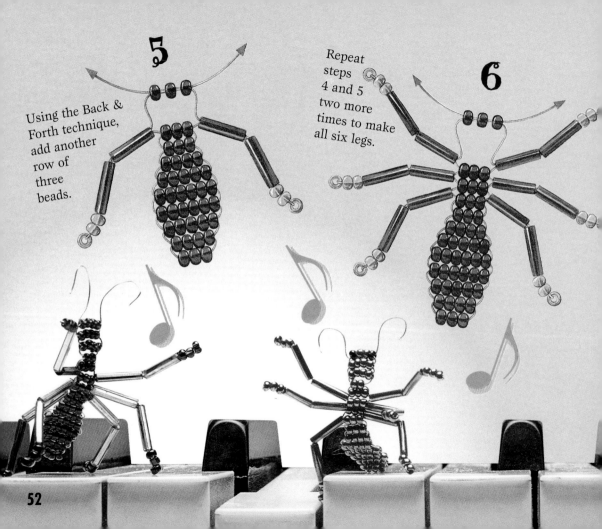

5

Using the Back & Forth technique, add another row of three beads.

6

Repeat steps 4 and 5 two more times to make all six legs.

7

Again with the Back & Forth technique, bead on four more rows following the bead count. Don't forget the eyes on the last row!

Clip the wires evenly and shape the antennae. We'll leave it up to you to give your dancin' ant a fancy pose.

Clip the wires evenly and shape the antennae.

4
4
4
2

Cha, Cha, Cha...

GRASSHOPPER

1 String seven green seed beads on the center of a 30″ piece of wire. Thread wire **A** back through four seed beads like this:

2 Using the Back & Forth technique, bead on the next eight rows following this pattern (the last row is a bugle bead):

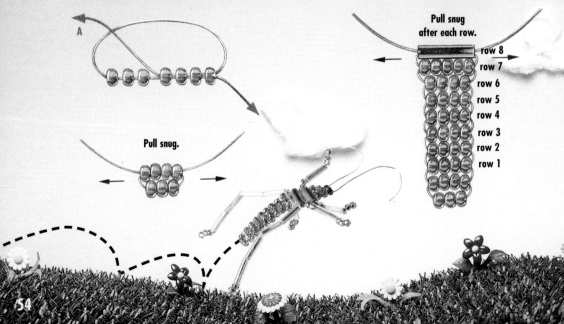

A

Pull snug.

Pull snug after each row.

row 8
row 7
row 6
row 5
row 4
row 3
row 2
row 1

For the back legs, string on four bugle beads and three seed beads on wire **A**.

Loop wire **A** around the last seed bead and thread it back through the leg beads like this:

Repeat step 3 for the other back leg.

A

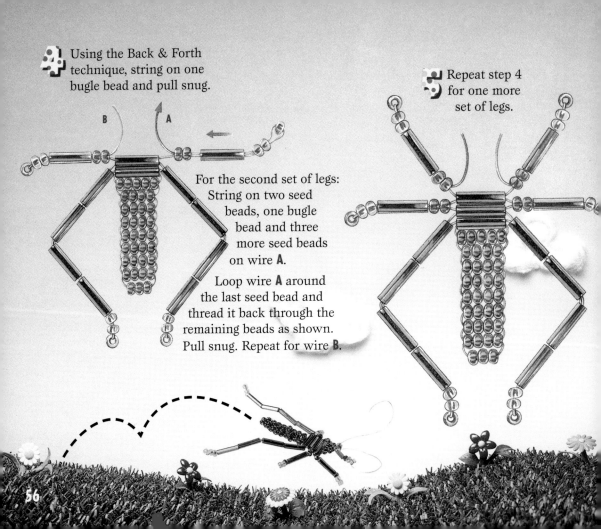

4 Using the Back & Forth technique, string on one bugle bead and pull snug.

B   A

5 Repeat step 4 for one more set of legs.

For the second set of legs: String on two seed beads, one bugle bead and three more seed beads on wire **A**.

Loop wire **A** around the last seed bead and thread it back through the remaining beads as shown. Pull snug. Repeat for wire **B**.

Using the Back & Forth technique, bead on the next four rows.

To finish, clip the wire ends (not too short!) and shape them into antennae.

4 4 3

People, People,
People

Girls

String seven seed beads on the center of a 24″ wire. Thread wire **A** back through the four beads as shown.

3 String four seed beads on wire **B**. Loop wire **B** around the last seed bead and back through the next three beads.

B

B

Pull snug.

Pull wire to snug beads.

2 Using the Back & Forth technique, bead on the next row following the pattern.

Repeat step 3 for wire **A**.

A

Pull snug.

Pull snug.

4

Using the Back & Forth technique, bead on the next two rows following this pattern:

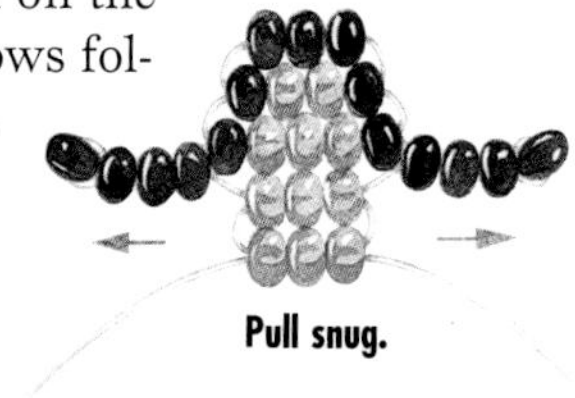

Pull snug.

5

String seven seed beads on wire **B**.

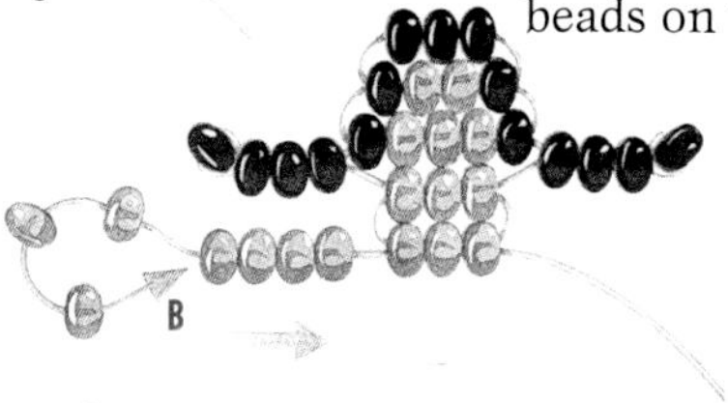

Loop the end of wire **B** around three seed beads and thread back through the next four beads as shown.

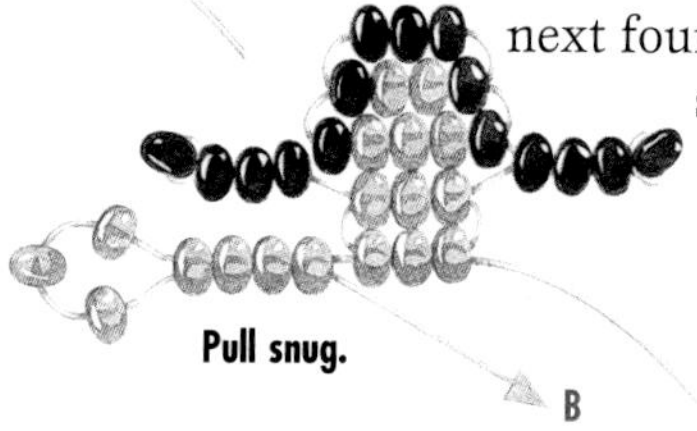

Pull snug.

B

Repeat for wire **A**.

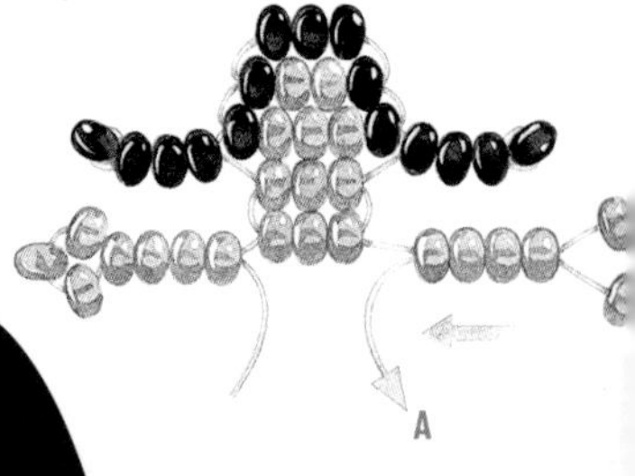

A

8 While your wires are still loose, thread a new piece of wire 10" long through the four center beads.

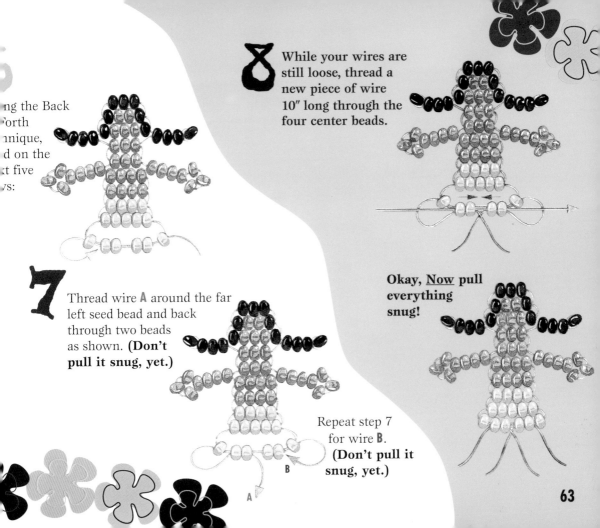

ng the Back
orth
nnique,
d on the
t five
s:

7 Thread wire **A** around the far left seed bead and back through two beads as shown. **(Don't pull it snug, yet.)**

Repeat step 7 for wire **B**. **(Don't pull it snug, yet.)**

B

A

Okay, <u>Now</u> pull everything snug!

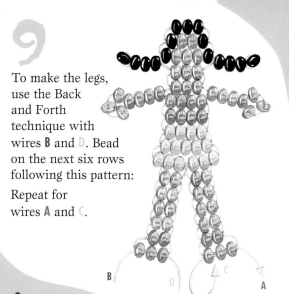

9

To make the legs, use the Back and Forth technique with wires **B** and **D**. Bead on the next six rows following this pattern:

Repeat for wires **A** and **C**.

B   D   C   A

TA DA!

Finishing Touch

A

C

Clip.

To finish off the foot, loop the end of wire **C** around the heel seed bead and out through the toe.

Thread wire **A** back through the ankle as shown. Clip the excess wire.

Repeat for the left leg.

Clip.

Try out these variations

Girls Girls Girls

Try this flowing skirt and matching purse ensemble.
By using the Back & Forth technique, it's easy to make the skirt. (Add some extra beads on the bottom rows to make the skirt flare out.) The purse is also easy to make with just four Back & Forth rows and a curved handle.

To make pants on your beaded girl, just follow the instructions for the **boy** steps 4 through to the finishing touch (pages 67–68).

For a stunning sarong, bead a long skirt following this bead pattern. With the Back & Forth technique, it's a snap!

For a stylish hairdo. bead your girl's head like this one, without hair. Then when you're done, wire some braided embroidery floss on top to make hair.

65

Oh Boy!

String seven seed beads on the center of a 24" wire.

1 Thread wire **A** back through four beads.

Like this:

B

A

Don't forget to pull the wire ends snug!

Pull snug.

2 Using the Back & Forth technique, bead on the next three rows following the pattern.

Pull snug after each row.

String seven seed beads on wire **A**.

Loop the end of wire **A** around three seed beads and thread it back through the next four seed beads as shown.

Pull snug.

Do the same on wire **B**.

Using the Back & Forth technique, bead on the next four rows following the pattern:

Loop wire **A** around the outside seed bead and back through one bead to the center.
Repeat for wire **B**.
Pull the wires snug.

Keep wires A and B crossed.

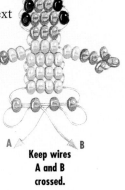

Cut a new wire 10″ long. Thread it through the four beads as shown.

6 To make the pants, begin with wires **B** and **C**. Using the Back & Forth technique, make five rows of two blue beads. Repeat for wires **A** and **D**.

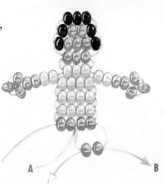

D   A   B
C

7 To make the shoes, add one row of two green beads, and then a row of three green beads.

Finishing Touch

B
C

To end, thread wire **B** back through the second to last row.

Loop wire C around the heel bead and out through the other two toe beads. Repeat for the other foot.

Clip.

Clip.

Boy! Oh Boy!

Try out these boy variations!

Want to give your boy a summer outfit? Try making shorts like these. All you need to do is add an extra bead to the third row of both legs.

For a stylish hairdo, thread a piece of wire through the top beads of your boy's head and give it a couple of tight twists. Cut ten strands of any color embroidery floss (a 2" length works well).

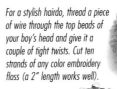

Wrap the wire ends tightly around the center of your floss pieces. Twist the wire ends a few times and clip off the excess wire. With scissors, give your boy a snappy haircut.

ANGEL

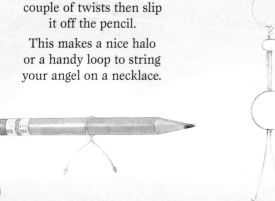

1

Cut 20" of wire.

Loop the center around a round pencil. Give it a couple of twists then slip it off the pencil.

This makes a nice halo or a handy loop to string your angel on a necklace.

2

String one clear seed bead and one large wonder bead onto both wires.

Slide the beads up close to the loop.

3

String three clear beads on wire **A**.

Thread wire **B** through the beads in the opposite direction as shown.

Pull both wires snug to center the beads under the wonder bead.

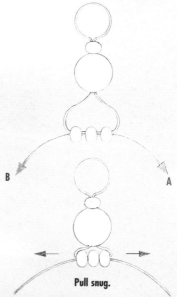

B   A

Pull snug.

4

String the wing beads (ten clear seed beads, one bugle, one clear seed bead, one bugle) on wire **A** following the pattern.

Thread the end of wire **A** back through the first seed bead as shown. Pull snug.

Repeat step 4 for wire **B**.

Now shape them into wings.

5

Using the Back & Forth technique, bead on the next eight rows following the pattern.

To finish, thread wire ends back through a row of beads.

Pull snug and clip the extra wire.

halo loop gets
d out of shape
st reshape it
th your pencil.

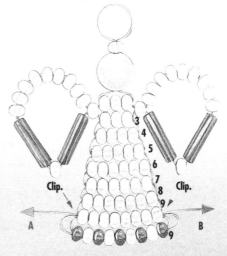

71

Mermaids
&
Friends

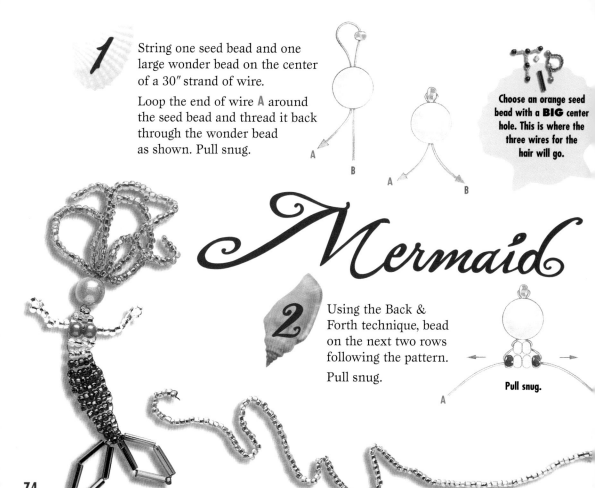

1 String one seed bead and one large wonder bead on the center of a 30″ strand of wire.

Loop the end of wire **A** around the seed bead and thread it back through the wonder bead as shown. Pull snug.

Choose an orange seed bead with a **BIG** center hole. This is where the three wires for the hair will go.

Mermaid

2 Using the Back & Forth technique, bead on the next two rows following the pattern.

Pull snug.

Pull snug.

4 String two small wonder beads on wire **A**.

Thread wire **B** through the beads in the opposite direction.

Pull snug.

B   A

3 String ten clear seed beads on wire **A**. Loop the end of wire **A** around the last three beads and thread it back through the remaining seven beads as shown.

Pull snug.

Hold the arm beads close to the body as you pull snug.

Repeat on wire **B**.

A   B

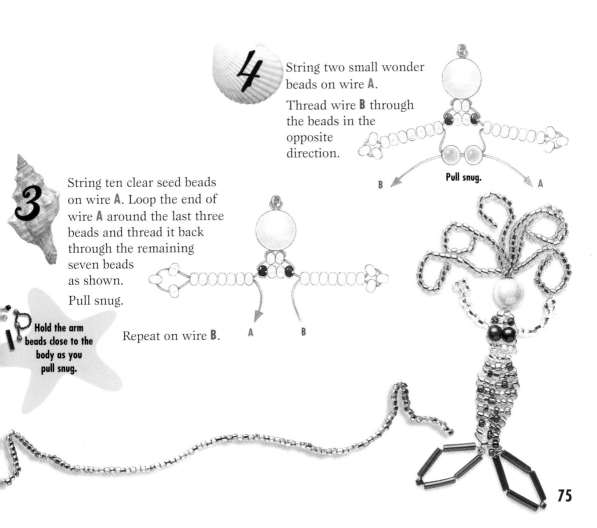

5

4
6
6
7
7
6
6
5
4
4
3
3

Using the Back & Forth technique, bead on the next 13 rows. Use whatever color combinations you want.

Pull snug after each row.

6

On wire **A**, string on the tail beads in this order: two bugle beads, one seed bead, and two more bugle beads. Thread the end of wire **A** back through the seed bead as shown. Pull snug. Repeat for wire **B**.

To finish, thread wires back through the second-to-last body bead row. Don't forget to clip the extra wire ends.

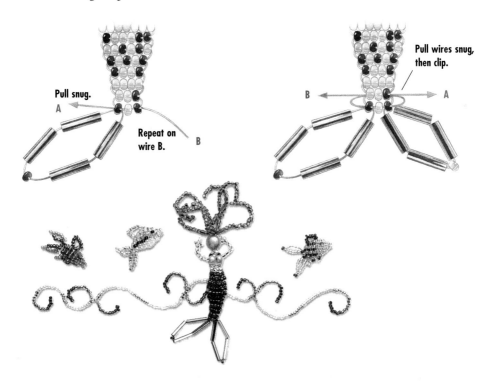

Pull snug.
A

Repeat on wire B.
B

Pull wires snug, then clip.

B ← → A

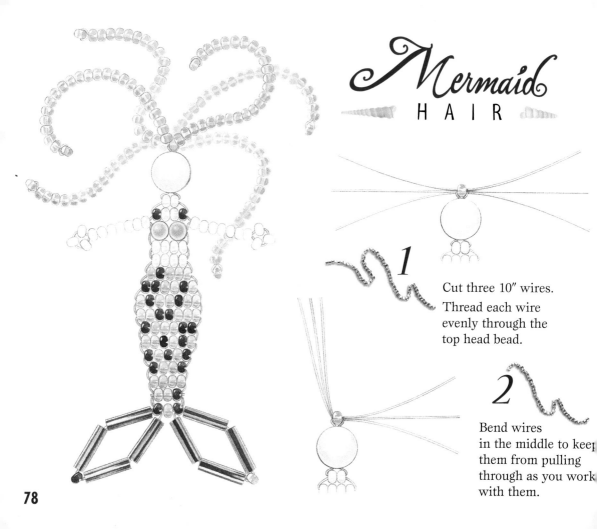

Mermaid
H A I R

1
Cut three 10″ wires.
Thread each wire
evenly through the
top head bead.

2
Bend wires
in the middle to keep
them from pulling
through as you work
with them.

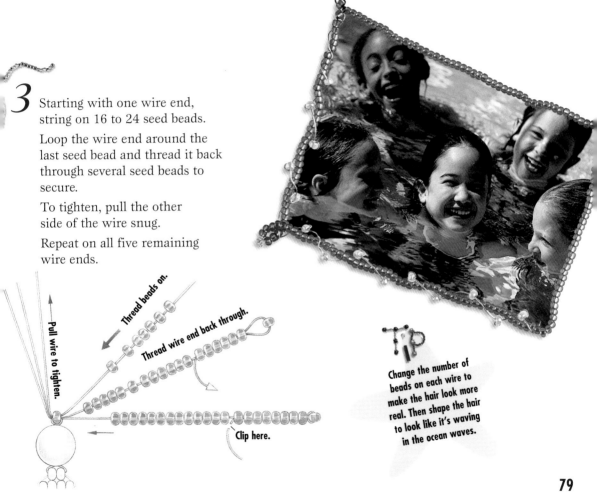

3 Starting with one wire end, string on 16 to 24 seed beads.

Loop the wire end around the last seed bead and thread it back through several seed beads to secure.

To tighten, pull the other side of the wire snug.

Repeat on all five remaining wire ends.

Thread beads on.

Thread wire end back through.

Pull wire to tighten.

Clip here.

TIP

Change the number of beads on each wire to make the hair look more real. Then shape the hair to look like it's waving in the ocean waves.

79

 **ropical Fish**

1 String five seed beads on the center of 18" of wire.

Thread wire **A** back through three beads like this:

Pull snug.

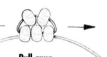

2 Using the Back & Forth technique, bead on the next three rows following this pattern:

Pull snug after each row.

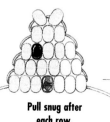

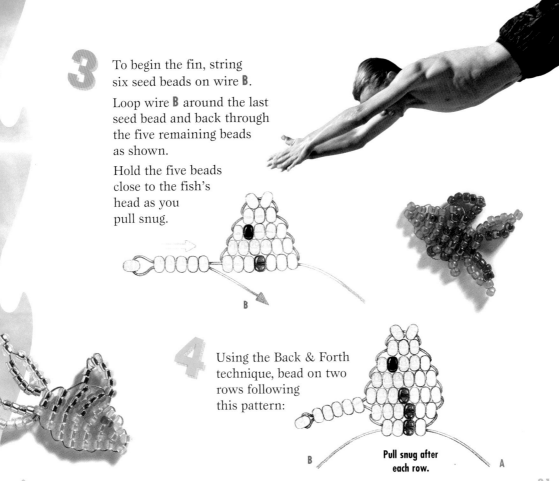

3 To begin the fin, string six seed beads on wire **B**.

Loop wire **B** around the last seed bead and back through the five remaining beads as shown.

Hold the five beads close to the fish's head as you pull snug.

B

4 Using the Back & Forth technique, bead on two rows following this pattern:

B

Pull snug after each row.

A

81

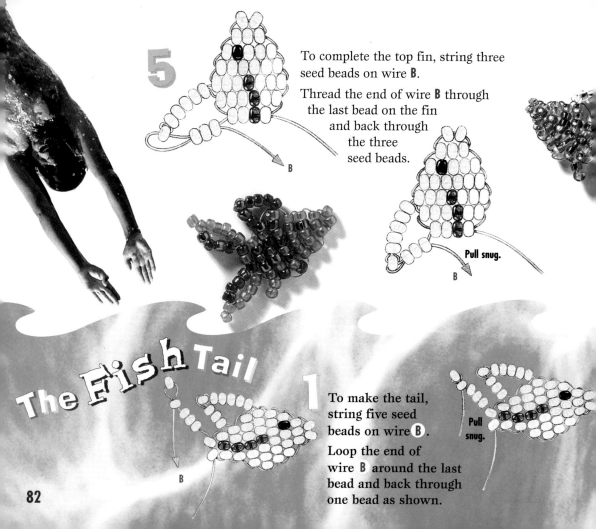

5

To complete the top fin, string three seed beads on wire **B**.

Thread the end of wire **B** through the last bead on the fin and back through the three seed beads.

Pull snug.

B

The Fish Tail

1

To make the tail, string five seed beads on wire **B**.

Loop the end of wire **B** around the last bead and back through one bead as shown.

Pull snug.

6 Using the Back & Forth technique, bead on the next two rows following this pattern.

◄— Pull snug. —►

B

A

2 String four seed beads on wire **B**.

B

3 To finish, thread wire **B** back through one seed bead and then back through the body bead row as shown. Pull snug then clip the extra wire.

Clip.

4 Repeat **The Fish Tail** steps 1–3 on wire **A**.

83

1

Put a green bead at the center of a 16" piece of wire.
Thread wire **B** back through the bead like this:

B

Pull snug.

2

Now string nine lime beads on wire **A**.
Loop wire **A** around the last bead and back through the second-to-last bead.

B

A

Pull snug.

3

Using the same wire **A**, string on five lime beads and one green bead.

Loop the wire around the last bead and pull it tight.

4

B

A

Repeat steps 2 & 3 four more times to make all five legs. Leave off the last green bead on the fifth leg. Thread the end of wire **A** through the first green bead.

String two clear beads on wire **A**. Thread wire **A** through the next green bead as shown. Pull snug.

B

A

5

Continue stringing on two clear beads between each green bead until the circle is completed. Pull snug.

Finishing Touch

Thread both wire ends back through two beads on the fifth leg. Pull snug. Clip extra wire.

Thread both wires through two beads.

Clip.

Starfish

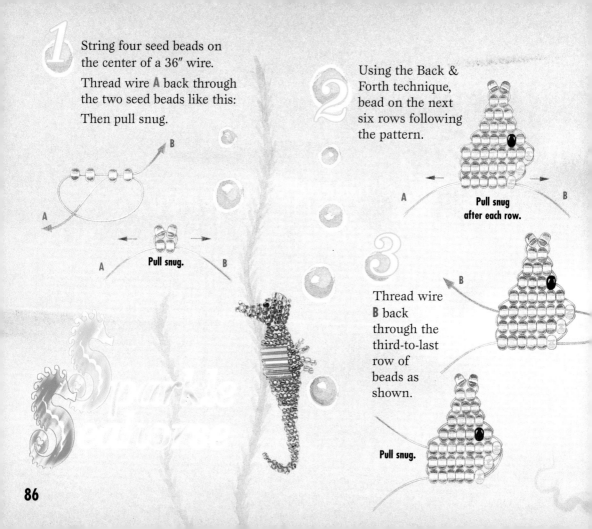

1 String four seed beads on the center of a 36" wire.

Thread wire **A** back through the two seed beads like this: Then pull snug.

Pull snug.

2 Using the Back & Forth technique, bead on the next six rows following the pattern.

Pull snug after each row.

3 Thread wire **B** back through the third-to-last row of beads as shown.

Pull snug.

86

Turn the head right side up and begin beading the body.

Using the Back & Forth technique, bead on the following pattern:

Pull snug after each row.

String two lime beads on wire **A**.

Loop wire **A** around the last seed bead and thread it back through the other lime bead as shown.

A

Pull snug.

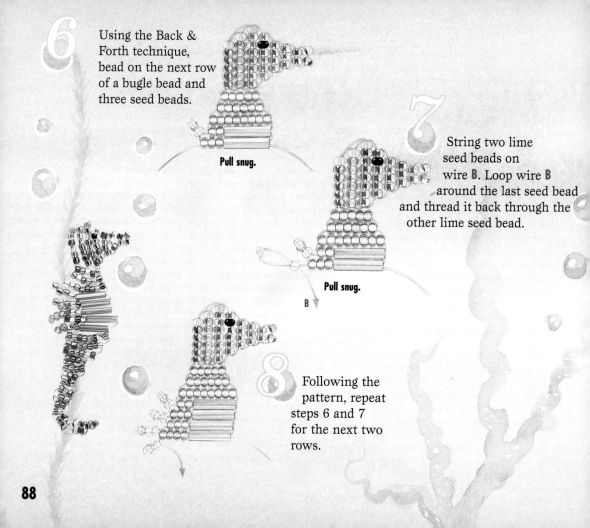

6 Using the Back & Forth technique, bead on the next row of a bugle bead and three seed beads.

Pull snug.

7 String two lime seed beads on wire **B**. Loop wire **B** around the last seed bead and thread it back through the other lime seed bead.

Pull snug.

B

8 Following the pattern, repeat steps 6 and 7 for the next two rows.

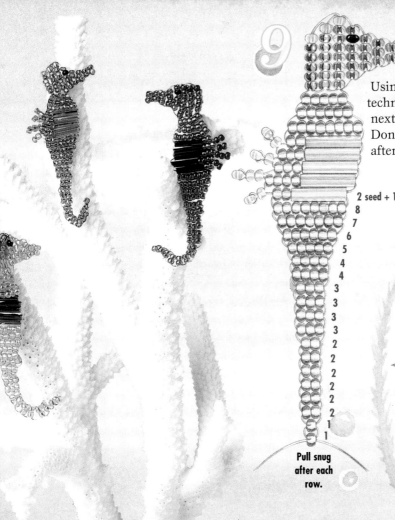

Using the Back & Forth technique, bead on the next 19 rows for the tail. Don't forget to pull snug after each row!

2 seed + 1 bugle bead

8
7
6
5
4
4
3
3
3
3
2
2
2
2
2
2
1
1

Pull snug after each row.

To secure the ends, thread the wire ends back through the second-to-last row.

finishing touch

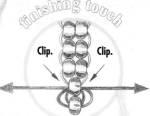

Clip.   Clip.

When you're done, curl up the tail of your sea-horse.

89

Book Designers: Jill Turney, Ellen Kwan

Cover Kibitzer: John Cassidy

Photographers: Peter Fox, Katrine Naleid,
Tomas Heinser, Jock McDonald

Photo Stylists: Bill Doggett, Jill Turney, Ellen Kwan

Illustrators: Darwen & Vally Hennings, Sara Boore, Ellen Kwan

Calligrapher: Nancy Hopkins

Model Wranglers: Corie Thompson, Susan Fox

Models: Jamie Lee Hurtt, Kim Ludlam, Kelsey Greenleaf,
Melissa Greenleaf, Laura Ferrari, Ahmad Sghayer, Jake Griffiths,
Pamela Wong, Jenner Fox, Fiona Beckner Kurtz, Charlie Wolfson,
Russ Frank, John Robert Frankfurt, Brent Almond,
Kaela Fox, Kolby Dauler, Michael Scott, Darius Johnson,
Rachel Williams, Natasha Johnson, Claire Anderton, Veronica
Prazdy-Dolan, Lainey Eaton, Miranda Erich, Tawny Pierce, Lily Vu,
Mislene Carlo, Rosa Yoshitsugu

Beaders: Lisa Lynch, Madeline Lynch, Molly McAndrew,
Keely Chanteloup, Connie Kuge, Candice Elton, Julie Collings,
Jill Turney, Corie Thompson, Laurie Campbell, Steve Kongsle,
Marilyn, Lynn & Herb Stacy, Valerie Traumuller

Thanks to our consultants for their inspiring ideas:
Katherine Van Cott, Tanji Johnson, Jacqueline Lee,
Laura Torres, Sherri Haab, Vicki Baum

Special Thanks to our kid inventors: Marina Collings,
Brigham and Rebekah Elton, Gavin Nichols, Rachel
and Michelle Haab

This book is dedicated to our families and especially
Matt and Rich for holding down the fort while we
wrote this book.

Who are you?

Name: _____ Age:_____ ❑ Too high to count ◯ Boy ◯ Girl

Address: _____ Phone (____)_____

City:_____ State: _____ Zip: _____

E-mail Address:_____

When I'm not reading Klutz books, my favorite thing to do is:_____

True or False!

❑ **T** ❑ **F** Someone gave me this book as a gift because they like me a whole lot!

❑ **T** ❑ **F** I bought this book for myself because I deserve it!

How did you first hear about this book?
◯ Friend ◯ Store shelf ◯ Store clerk ◯ In a Klutz book ◯ Other

❑ **T** ❑ **F** This is the first Klutz book I've ever bought/received.

My Bright Ideas!

Tell us what you think of this book:_____

_____

What would you like us to write a book about? _____

❑ Check this box if you want us to send you The Klutz Catalog.

Beadlings™

KLUTZ®

455 Portage Avenue
Palo Alto, CA 94306